BLAME IT ON THE TEXAS SKY

MAX MUNDAN

Blame it on the Texas Sky
Max Mundan

ISBN: 978-1-948712-38-5

© 2019 Max Mundan
Cover Design by Thyra Rutter

Weasel Press
Manvel, TX
www.weaselpress.com

Printed in the U.S.A.

ALL RIGHTS RESERVED. This book contains material protected under International and Federal Copyright Laws and Treaties. Any unauthorized reprint or use of this material is prohibited. No part of this book, or use of characters in this book, may be reproduced or transmitted in any form or by any means, electronic or mechanical, including photocopying, recording, or by any information storage and retrieval system without expressed written permission from the author / publisher, except for review and educational purposes.

CONTENTS

Blame It On the Texas Sky	1
Between First and Slaughter	3
Her Valley Story	5
Going Through the Motions	7
When You Look in the Mirror (and you're not there)	9
Sheila Told Me	11
Running for My Life (in Freedom, California)	13
Dyin' On the 405	15
Cheap Motel Room Blues	17
Limp Dick Stare	19
Lisa Was	21
Slipping Back	23
Happy When	25
What is This Despare?	27
A Junkie's Field Guide to California Toilets	29
Quality Time	31
All the Pretty Children	33
Still an Asshole	35
Pragmatic Jane	37
Waiting in the Methadone Line	38
One Bloody Christmas	41
Weirder than He Looks	44
Black and Blue Mass	46
Devil in the Details	48
A Quality of Mercy	52
How To Broach the Subject of Anal with the Woman of your Dreams	54
Sympathy for the Dealer	56
Everything's MacBeth	58
The Pathology of need and Night Train	59
At the Capitol Garden Motel	61
How to Explain Karma to a Small Child	63
1996	65

Best Laid Plans	66
Sex or Suicide	68
There Ain't Epiphany Enough for That	69
The Lie	70
Walls are Thin	74
Wasted Life	76
One Drop of Milk	78
Passing the Torch	80
Words Spoken, and Words Left Unsaid	82
This Space	84
Alienation Songs	85
Death Watch	87
Long Winter	89
Cock and Consequence	91
Pity	92
The Spiritual Derivation of the Word "Fuck"	95
Don't Go Away	97
Allow Me To Break the Fourth wall and Speak to You, The Reader, Directly	99
Busy Fucking the Rat Girl	101
To the Girl with Armageddon in Her Eyes	104
Lousy Bouncer	107
Criminal	109
The Graces of Dian	112
Searching for Jesus (On the World.Wide.Web)	113
Diane's First Abortion	115
Great Moments in Silence	116
Memento Mori	117
Linda's Choice	118
Acid and You and Allen Ginsberg	120

To the fathers and mothers, the brothers and sisters, the husbands, wives and lovers of Teilhard, of Lisa, of Click and of Jim. It wasn't your fault. It was never your fault.

BLAME IT ON THE TEXAS SKY

BLAME IT ON THE TEXAS SKY

Chelsea said to me one night,
"I am the Alamo, you know?"
and before I could ask her
what the hell she meant by that
she continued, 'I've got a thousand men
who want to defend me,
who will try to defend me,
who would lay down their lives
to defend me, but in the end,
I'm going to fall, and there is nothing
they can do to stop it."

And I began to tell her
that was stupid, that was silly,
that she was going to be just fine
and was going to make one of those men
a wonderful wife someday,
but I couldn't get the words
out of my mouth because I knew
they were bullshit and so, instead,
I said to her, "Why do you think that is?"

Chelsea didn't answer right away but,
instead, she played with the little
drops of blood that were pouring
from the crook of her arm,
making a little smiley face
on my copy of the Big Book
that was sitting right in front of her.

Finally, she looked up at me
with those eyes that screamed genocide
and responded, "Who the hell knows?
It's my parent's fault. It's Nixon's fault.

2

It's Marlene Dietrich's fault. Something
must have made me this way. Shit,
blame it on the Texas sky
for all I care."

And with that, she put her head
in my lap and wiped her tears, absently,
on my erection. It was her way
of telling me, "Give it up, boy.
I know you want to fix me, too,
but it's gonna take a better tool
than the one you got there."

BETWEEN FIRST AND SLAUGHTER

Susie had lived
on a rat-eaten blanket
on the sidewalks of Main Street,
between First and Slaughter

She was 97 pounds
of bad language and bile
but she hadn't the muscle
to fight off the crack-heads and junkies
who needed her body
to keep warm at night

Since Susie'd blown out her veins
before hitting the street,
she'd been shooting
in the fat of her stomach
She'd hoped that the smell
would deter the bad men
but their type
was not so easily discouraged

When she'd begun to ooze
green pus and red blood,
a regular downtown Christmas,
she was fresh out of millionaire benefactors
and affordable insurance
to get it taken care of

This morning,
when Austin came to pick me up,
where I was waiting,
between First and Slaughter,
he pointed to the filthy blanket
tied up in a ball and asked me,

4

"What the hell's that?"

"That's Susie," I answered,
"and she didn't matter,
to anyone."

HER VALLEY STORY

She had no more friends
who could wipe her brow
and wipe her ass
and chop the crystal meth for her
into tiny, little lines

She had no more friends
who could burn her bacon
and call her pretty
and carry her up and down
the stairs when her legs failed

This was her valley story
because her parents were the mountains
and she was sentenced to exile
in the prison of her body

She had no more friends
who could drive her to the market
and drive her out of her mind
and clean up the blood when she
smashed her face on the nightstand

She had no more friends
she could call "fucker"
and "asshole" and "stupid son of a bitch"
after they'd cleaned her up
when she'd soiled herself in the bathroom

This was her valley story
because she'd been a waterfall
but now she was stale, lonely droplets
disappearing in the unforgiving sun

6

    This was her valley story
    because she's lost on the highway
    traveling from peace of mind
    to sad and pointless death

    alone in a room
    alone in a room
    alone in a room

    about six weeks
    after the last of her lovers
    had ceased
    to give a damn

GOING THROUGH THE MOTIONS

Dana only wanted me
to fuck her
She didn't like me
sucking her pussy
She wanted to save something special
just for her boyfriend
That's what she told me
and, if you want to know the truth
I didn't really give a damn
The only thing I'd been doing
down between her legs
was showing off
I was perfectly happy
to save the effort
and the energy

When I first met Dana
she gave me a look that says,
"You may have fooled the others
but you don't fool me
and if you promise not to waste my precious time
with bon mots and attempts at wit
then you can fuck me
till you're blue in the face."

I know that look
I've seen that look before

and fuck we did
over and over
for several weeks one summer
that felt like a year
and we somehow managed to hide the rutting
from the wonderful people

to whom we'd promised to be faithful

So we went at each other
day after day
with acrobatic, if joyless, precision

Strip the clothes
hit the bed
thrust, roll, fuck
disengage
then hide the evidence

and, in the end, it was obvious to me
that what Dana and I were doing
had very little to do
with trying to make each other cum
This was sex as penance
It was just to prove
to the world
to ourselves
that we weren't worthy
of being loved

WHEN YOU LOOK IN THE MIRROR
(AND YOU'RE NOT THERE)

Someone is staring
back at you

someone you knew
you would never become

Are you crying?
Is that a tear
rolling down your face?
Do you miss the one
you were hoping to see?

I remember the first time
the first time
that I fucked somebody
I didn't want to fuck
I let them run
their course, ugly hands
all over my smooth body
let them shove
their sour, sullen tongue
deep into my mouth
while I tried
not to gag
not to choke
and then I smiled
a big, wide, bullshit lie of a smile
while they mounted me
so intent
on the satisfaction of their lust
never bothering to notice
my eyes
which were begging

pleading
for them to see
the real me

Are you crying?
Or are your eyes
dry?
Have you forgotten
the face
you were praying
to see?

Still, someone is staring
back at you

Someone you knew
you would never become

SHEILA TOLD ME

Sheila told me that she wasn't bound
by any bourgeois, suburban
standard of beauty; that she
could put on as much weight
as she desired and shave her head
and grow the hair out on her legs
and no stuck-up, normie bitches
were going to tell her
that she wasn't hot.

Sheila told me that she would stay out
till 4 in the morning, every night,
dancing and fucking and laughing
and shooting crystal meth
because those were the only things
that made her feel that she
was really alive and not some
stupid Barbie Doll being
made up and dressed up
and moved around by forces
she could never see or understand.

Sheila told me that sex was power
and if I wanted, she could teach me
to use my dick the way
she used her pussy, as a weapon,
a trap to lure the squares,
the suits and ties and frat boys
who laughed at her and called
her ugly, called her fat,
called her weirdo, but never failed
to come sniffing at her ass
when they thought no one was looking.

Sheila told me that she didn't
want to live past forty; that
an aging life was an unartful life
and that she wasn't meant
for wrinkles and eye bags and
sagging tits and regret; that
the saddest dopes were the ones
who just kept going, taking
up space and sucking up air
after everyone they'd ever known
had died or long since ceased
to give a shit.

Sheila told me that she'd call me
if she ever decided to do
anything stupid,

but Sheila never called.

RUNNING FOR MY LIFE (IN FREEDOM, CALIFORNIA)

The siren is like a drill
carving a hole in my skull
and the red and blue, flashing
in my rear-view mirror,
is making it difficult
to focus on the road in front of me.

I've got two balloons
full of black tar heroin,
the pride of Chiang Mai,
hidden under the butts
at the bottom of my ashtray,
but the police will take one look
at the track marks all down my arms
and tear this car apart.

I shouldn't have run that red light
but I'm pouring sweat and the fear
is making my teeth rattle
like a bucket full of marbles.
I need a hit bad and
I was just trying to get home.

Probably shouldn't have painted
"Fuck the Police" on the side of the car, either.
I can't imagine that they'll take it
in a nice and friendly way.
Unless I miss my guess,
my political statement should be good
for a night-stick across the ribs,
if not a good, old-fashioned beat down.

I swallow both of the balloons
and push the pedal to the floor

as I get myself prepared
for cold turkey in a hot, cement cell,
because it's just another night in Freedom, California
running from the cops.

DYIN' ON THE 405

We've only just passed Sunset Boulevard,
doing about 2 miles an hour the entire way,
and we've been in this traffic for 45 minutes now,
Penelope and I, and I have to believe
that I'm going to crawl out of my skin
because my house is in the Valley
and the dope is in my pocket,

where it isn't doing anybody
any good at all.

I hate this city of Angels sometimes
because when you live in Encino
and the dealer, he's in Westwood,
you can get sick just tryin' to score
and the sign up ahead says a mile more
to Getty Center Dr. and the traffic creeps
slower than the beads of sweat,

that roll down my face and drop
on my shirt.

And I feel the fear now, beginning
to claw its way up my spine, because
I know we've still got Mulholland
and then Ventura, before we even reach
the 101, and my nose is starting to run
and I can feel my bowels beginning
to loosen and churn, so that I'm worried

I won't make it home before
I shit my pants.

Penelope starts to whine now, and I know

she feels it too, because she makes a sound
like her soul is being sucked out
through her face, which has gone
completely white, the same as mine,
I'm sure, but it's still half a mile
to the Getty and the odds are looking good

that we'll never got off
this fucking freeway.

CHEAP MOTEL ROOM BLUES

Your distinctive aroma lingers on me
on my chest, in my hair
on my dick
all over my dick
There is little chance
that she will fail to notice
I must find a place
to wash what's left of you from me
to erase your memory
before I go home
to her

Lying next to her in bed
feeling the expectant heat
of her body pressing mine
there is so much to say
to you
to you
only to you
for her I have nothing
but disappointment and excuses
lies, lies, so many lies
Life can be so cruel
sometimes I can be so cruel
sometimes

Does getting my needs met
always mean
that someone else
has theirs
ripped away?

Another day, another room
and you

wet, warm and willing
We shed our guilt and our shame
just like our clothes
and leave them lying on the floor
in careless piles
Only later, when we part ways
will we pick them up again
to wear under our garments
like a hair shirt

I want to dress you up
in trappings and shrouds
knit out of stars
I pulled down from the sky
but all I have to give you
is my sweat
and my cum
and my apologies

LIMP DICK STARE

Roger lifted his eyes to Sarah's
and looked at her with that insufferable
limp dick stare of his
and rifled through his laundry list of excuses-

I was drunk and didn't know
what I was doing, or

it was after midnight and I thought
for sure she was you, or

you never told me
monogamy was expected, or

I tripped and my cock
just fell into your sister.

When he saw the look
on Sarah's face, however,
he decided it was smarter
to keep his mouth shut.

He spent the next two days
walking on eggshells and pretending
her Sylvia Plath romantics
were just the silence
of a curious mind.

"She'll snap out," he told himself,
just like she had with Rachel
and Elizabeth before that
or when he'd sold her wedding dress
to pay his gambling debt.,
"She'll forget and then move on."

So, it surprised him when, on Sunday,
he walked into the living room to find
that Sarah had taken a rope
and a stool and decided to make
one final test of
the theory of gravity.

Roger considered the mess
swaying gently in front of him
and thought, "Damn, that's a shame.
Two more months and we'd
have paid off the car.
Where in hell am I going to find
the money to do it now?"

LISA WAS

Lisa was wild smiles and spontaneity
cascading laughter skipping stumbling
down the street and Lisa was one
long string of piss-fucking-poor decisions

Lisa was my friend
Lisa was
my friend
Lisa was

Lisa was the apple of her mother's eye
awkwardly growing too tall and all
ankles and knees and elbows and Lisa was
nights awake wondering if she was alive

Lisa was a daughter
Lisa was
a daughter
Lisa was

Lisa was the lifetime love of many men
crazy and fickle and impossible to hold
lust and need and whiskey breath and Lisa was
dead weight her boys would try to drag from bed

Lisa was a wife
Lisa was
a mother
Lisa was

Lisa was track marks and second chances
pus-filled wounds hidden under blouses
broken promises lying promises and Lisa was
a cold and rigid form beneath a sheet

Lisa was an addict
Lisa was
a junkie
Lisa was

SLIPPING BACK

I watched over her while she kicked dope
sweating and
       twitching and
              screaming obscenities
                      "Fuck you and all your holier than thou
                              bullshit, "she said
She promised me
it was going to be the last time
that she would screw up this bad
and who was I to judge?
I tried to drag her from the jaws of death
but she just kept
slipping back

I sat by her at the doctor's
all the blood and
       the pus and
              the nose burning stench
                        as he lanced one abscess after
                            another
I had never
seen someone I cared about
in this much pain before
but what choice did I have?
I was trying to pull her from the gutter
but she just kept
slipping back

You know, I told myself
I loved her but I didn't know
what that word even meant
She was just my new addiction
and the purpose and power I felt
was what was really in my grip

when I thought I was holding
her hand

I listened when she relapsed
as she lied
        and she lied
                through her teeth
                        that she was sober, that she
                              was clean

I didn't want
to push her out
of my life forever
but that's exactly what I did
Instead of me, lifting her up
she was only
dragging me down
so I let go of her hands
and watched her disappear
as she just kept
slipping back

HAPPY WHEN

Elaine knew she'd be happy when
she got off the junk and the needle
went back to only drinking with friends
and smoking a little pot at parties
she wouldn't be sick all the time
and need to fuck disgusting, dirty assholes
to make it through another day
and get enough money
to keep her habit going

Elaine knew she'd be happy when
she finally met her Prince Charming
a real man with a good job
who would make her feel like someone special
and sweep her off her feet
to a life of luxury and ease
a nice man, a good man
instead of another bad boy loser
one of a series of drunken abusers
who, once they'd fucked her and punched her
a time or two
was out the door and on the prowl
for the next victim or hostage

Elaine knew she'd be happy when
she got that one great acting job
that was waiting, right around the corner
just out of reach
because, after all, she was as good
as talented, as sexy, as willing
as any other bitch out there
and if she had to do some things
sacrifice a little dignity
give up a moral here

or an ethic there
then she was down for that too

She'd gladly throw away
any piece of herself
if it could make her
happy

Elaine knew she'd be happy when
she got her shit together
and all the vampires out of her life
because it wasn't her fault she was depressed
it was them, all of them
all those fuckers conspiring against her
keeping her down
if they'd only leave her alone
stop tempting and taunting her
convincing her to indulge
her darkest desires and to succumb
to her pathetic weakness

Elaine knew she'd be happy when
she was no longer
so
fucking
miserable
but what should she do
when being unhappy
was the only thing
she was good at?

WHAT IS THIS DESPARE?
(*for Chris Cornell*)

It whispers in my ear,
"You cannot win, you cannot win."
and plies me with oily fingers
that squeeze my balls
and scrape sharp nails down my cock,
reveling in my discomfort.

"It feels like sex to you,"
it tells me, "This failure.
This weakness of the will."
It knows that what I am
is a screaming, white-hot orb
of anger and loss
and that I'll never be more.

What is this
need, that promises redemption
then only delivers
a vacuum?

What is this
dismay, this melancholy truth
that owns the key
to my heart?

I want to quit and I want to quit and I
can't and I want to quit and I want to
quit and I can't and I want to quit and
I want to quit and I can't and I want

and I want

and I want

and I want

and I can't

continue.

A JUNKIE'S FIELD GUIDE TO CALIFORNIA TOILETS

This is the temple, the tabernacle
this is the sacristy
and the quiet here, the empty
is chocolate-covered cotton-candy
it's marshmallow pillows
it's Saturday morning cartoons
it's Mommy's distant womb
you can hear a pin drop
or at least a needle
and so it does
the needle drops
this is good

I remember driving the length of California with my family and, Jesus Christ, was I sick. We'd been traveling for hours and the dope I had shot before we'd left had worn off. I needed to find a bathroom badly. So I could shoot up with a little fucking peace. Not so many goddamn prying eyes. The best that you can find is one of those one-person bathrooms, with a door that locks, and it's just you and the needle and the silence. That is golden, baby. You can bleed all over the walls and no one will ever know. At least no one in the family. A stall with a door is the bare minimum. if you find one of the run-down places where the doors have fallen off or don't lock, then you are fucked. Naturally, this is what happened. I held the door shut with my foot, while I tied-off with my hands and teeth, holding the tourniquet in my mouth. It took me so long, trying to find a vein and maintain my barricade that my father came and pounded on the door, demanding to know what was taking me so long. I ended up having to give up, put the heroin in my mouth and chew, just to get a little bit into my system.

This is my spaceship, my cubbyhole
this is my ferry down the Styx

the peace here, it breaks my heart
it's tears of barbed wire
it's oatmeal made of glass
it's champagne flutes filled with cyanide
it's my little baby's smile
the ground here is consecrated
to offer my sacrament
and so I do
on hands and knees
I offer praise

At a huge dinner in San Francisco, I snuck away to the bathroom to find that the stalls had little, swinging saloon doors, like in the old west. What the fuck were they thinking when they built this place? How is someone supposed to take a shit here, let alone shoot some black tar into their arm. I had to make up a crazy lie. I whispered into my father's ear that I had hemorrhoids and needed to go back to the car to get my medicine. No, it couldn't fucking wait. I had to go now. I know he didn't believe me and everyone knew exactly where I was going and what I was doing but at this point, we were all still trying to pretend that I was still their good, little boy, so he gave me the keys to the car and watched me walk out the door. He told me later that he wasn't sure he was ever going to see me again. At least not alive.

This is the confessional
I can hear the priest breathing
on the other side of the door
it's the waiting room to the slaughterhouse
it's the last meal in limbo
it's the grains in the hourglass
slowly sliding out
when I shut the door
this is who I really am
without pretense, without guile
without any hope of salvation

QUALITY TIME

Snorting coke off the toilet seat
in Aunt Connie's bathroom,
I think about my clueless family,
sharing hugs and telling jokes,
on the other side of the door.

I'd like so much to join them
in their warmth and good feeling
but I'm a shit
who doesn't give a damn
about any but myself
and I cannot look them
in the eyes.

I was awake all night,
with my head buried
in a pile of white powder,
and between the tits
of a cheap but talented whore.
Once every hour or so
I would remember my family
and how it would break their tender hearts
to see me in this state,
but then I'd toot another line
and push them from my mind.

Now, careening wildly from the bathroom,
I crash, headfirst,
into the dinner table,
launching its contents across the room;
onto the walls;
onto their clothes;
onto their shocked and disappointed faces,
but I'm not done. No,

not by half, as I rear back,
convulsing uncontrollably,
before vomiting, in the mess
that I've created
of everything.

My mouth is open,
yet no sound comes out
and, as my tears drop over my lips,
burning my throat with their shame,
I croak the only words I can find
in my raw and fevered mind.
"This has been great," I say,
"We should do this again.
Real soon."

ALL THE PRETTY CHILDREN

All the pretty children
are dressing up
in the clothing that they chose
they don't care anymore
if you approve or disapprove
the pretty children know
their sexy smiles are sunbeams
that can cut through the midnight
of your restrictions

Arise, pretty children, arise
show us the glory of you
teach us the flow of the river

past the woman

and man

to what's next

All the pretty children
are going out
into the streets
that have been barred to them before
you can throw up your roadblocks
but the pretty children fly
high above them
on wings of loss and heartbreak
laughing at your sneers

Rejoice, pretty children, rejoice
love whosoever you please
your passion will never be limited

to the custom

the law

and the rule

All the pretty children
are lighting up
the cities of the night
with their burning hearts
and incandescent tear drops
the pretty children see
the barbed-wire in their paths
but refuse to admit
that it can make them bleed

You're free, pretty children, you're free
dance in the streets, if you please
your beauty cannot be held

in a jar

or a jail

or a fist

STILL AN ASSHOLE

Greg has been off the junk
for almost seven years now
He no longer needs to spend his days
hanging out at the needle exchange
or his nights
pistol whipping convenience store clerks
so he can pocket all the money from the till
Greg is clean
Greg is serene
but he's still a fucking asshole

Greg cannot remember the last time
he had forced a young, junkie girl
to give him a sloppy blowjob
for a little taste of dope
and his mother didn't need
to hide her purse anymore
every time he came to visit
Greg doesn't need to deal
Greg doesn't need to steal
but he's still a fucking asshole

Andy said to me one day,
"Do you know what Greg does?
He invites the newcomer girls
over to his house,
under the pretense of helping them work the steps,
but before you know it
he's got them stripped naked
and is teaching them recovery
with the business end of his dick."

I answered, "This surprises you, how?
He was an asshole as a junkie.

He is still an asshole now.
Greg is just a fucking asshole."

Anne said to me this morning,
"Greg promised that if I let him fuck me,
he'd make sure my boyfriend never found out,
but he's told every goddamn guy in the program
and now I can't show my face
at any of my meetings.
I thought clean people
were supposed to behave better."

So I said to her, "Getting sober
doesn't make you a better person.
He was an asshole as a user
He's still an asshole now
Greg's just a fucking asshole

Greg has only vague and distant memories
of embezzling money
from the nice guy he worked for
or selling straight baby laxative
to the sad and desperate street hypes
Greg doesn't need to lie anymore
Greg doesn't need to cheat anymore
He just does it 'cause he likes it
He is still a fucking asshole

PRAGMATIC JANE

Jane put down the hundred-dollar-bill
she was using to snort the small pile
of cocaine I had given her, then
she looked me straight in the eyes,
with an intense, burning power
I didn't have the courage to hold.

"Do you want to fuck me?" she asked,
then wet her finger with her tongue,
dabbed it in the pile of coke
and rubbed the powder all around her gums,
never once taking her eyes
off my face as she did so.

"That isn't necessary," I answered,
"I gave you that stuff
out of the goodness of my heart
and you don't owe me anything
to pay for it."

She looked at me for a minute
like I was a dead fish
that was smelling up the room
and said to me, "Uh huh,
I'm sure you're Prince Charming."

Then she pulled her shirt over her head
and threw it on the floor, as she told me,
"Look. I know this shit ain't free,
and I'd rather give you my cunt
than owe you any fucking gratitude."

WAITING IN THE METHADONE LINE

Sheila was waiting
waiting for the court
to give her kids back
to believe that she had given herself
to Jesus now and that she was walking
the straight and narrow
keeping her nose clean
staying off the dope
not turning tricks
and keeping creeps and con-men
out of her bed and out of her life
Sheila wanted them to think
that staying clean was more
more than a dog and pony show
but she knew damn well
that as soon as the kids got home
she was breaking out the needle
and the spoon
one more time
Sheila was waiting
waiting in the methadone line

Reggie was waiting
waiting for his wife
to get enough courage
to finally walk out on him
after all the shit he had pulled
and she had put up with
year after year after year
all the lies and all the promises
he had lost count ages ago
of all the times he had let her down
and she had threatened to leave
Reggie didn't care anymore

he couldn't remember
if he had loved her in the beginning
but he sure as hell
didn't love her now
and maybe if she left
he could get a little money
out of her
Reggie was waiting
waiting in the methadone line

Lizzie was waiting
waiting for her case
to just go away
she had been speeding down Sunset
high as a kite on large amounts
of very high-quality coke and smack
she hadn't a care in the world
until she hit that parked Chevy
going 85 miles an hour
and suddenly, everything in her life
changed for the worse
Lizzie was fine, believe it or not
too stoned to feel a thing
but her best friend Sue
in the passenger seat
never woke up from her coma
Liz had a billionaire daddy, though
who found a fancy lawyer
to get her out of trouble
Lizzie was waiting
waiting in the methadone line

And, I too, am waiting
waiting for my willpower
to die of neglect
I don't know how many times

I've tried to get clean
but I'd get two days or three days
before the fear and the rage
would gnaw at me
like a trapped rat
chewing off its own foot
and I'd be back on the street again
I didn't want to stop using, see
I just wanted to not have to
sell myself to lonely old perverts
or rip off my family
or hustle some poor slob
out of his hard-earned money
just to buy enough dope
to keep myself well
So here I am
Waiting
waiting in the methadone line

ONE BLOODY CHRISTMAS

My family, you are locked
away

on the other side of the bathroom door

and outside of my heart

I cannot let you in
if I am to survive
this Christmas
with my secret
intact

I want to embrace you
to love you
my blood
you are a part of me
what I wouldn't give
to curl up by the fire
to open the presents
to breath in the holiday
with you

but this disaster
this screaming need
is more important

I know you're knocking
calling my name
I can hear the worry in your voice
feel your fear
radiating
through the door

I cannot come out

You are my blood
and I love you
so acutely it burns in my gut
like a blowtorch

but in my rush
to appease my addiction
and return to your party
your Christmas
your side
I've pulled out the needle
before I loosened the tie
and now the blood in my veins
is spraying from me
like a fountain
painting the walls
in melancholy burgundy

tears well
in my eyes because
I don't know what to do

I'll never get this bathroom clean

My only choice
is to tell you some story
some lie
that you will never
truly
believe
but will keep you from asking
questions

This lie will seem familiar

it will be just like the others
I've sold to you
before

I'm sorry

You are my blood
but you can be washed away
and I'm afraid
that this blood

cannot

WEIRDER THAN HE LOOKS

Darren is weird
weirder than he looks
you can see it
deep in the quicksand
of his eyes

He doesn't need
       the black nail polish
He doesn't need
       the black mascara
He doesn't need
       the black lipstick
He doesn't need
       the black eyeliner
He's black
deep down in his soul

Darren might be smiling at you
but don't be deceived
he's trying to guess
how heavy you'll be
he's imagining the perfect place
to dispose of your body

He doesn't need
       the pink hair
He doesn't need
       the blue hair
He doesn't need
       the purple hair
He doesn't need
       the green hair
He's memorized your sins
and scribbles them down

in black and white

Darren once explained to me
in minute detail
how to build a bomb
that could level a small city
I don't believe
he'd ever actually make one
but I wouldn't bet my mother's life

He doesn't need
        to wear leather
He doesn't need
        to wear chains
He doesn't need
        to wear make-up
He doesn't need
        to wear platform shoes
His weird is deep inside him
it goes down
to the bone

Darren knew
the most effective way
to torture a man's genitals
and get him to tell you
anything you wanted to know
in the shortest amount of time
He would describe every step
in flat, calm, emotionless detail

Darren is weird
weirder than he looks
you can hear it
in the crime of passion
of his voice

BLACK AND BLUE MASS

arms entwined
legs wrapped
around backs
sweat mixing with
sweat, blood commingling
with blood
and saliva
and love
and loathing

for you
for me
forever

obliterate my borders
in the kingdom of you

hit me, kiss me, hit me
slap my tear-stained face
make me scream with
bitterness and bliss and rage

crack my skull
against your knee
snap my fingers
in your teeth

punch me

hard

harder

harder

so that I can't feel
the pain

DEVIL IN THE DETAILS

Listen carefully here
I'm trying to teach you something
Can't you see that?
What are you?
Some kind of idiot?
This shit is important
Every little thing
every detail
is important

You're going to want to keep
two lighters
with you at all times
in case of emergency
Say you're trying to cook
you got your spoon all prepared
and you run out of flame
If you ain't got a back up
you're fucked
know what I'm saying?
Don't be that guy
Think ahead, why don't you?

You getting all this?
You writing this stuff down?
You can learn a lot
from a man like me
Respect your elders
know what I'm saying?
You're just starting out
but I've been around the block
a time or two
or three or four or five

Do a few jumping jacks
ten or twenty
something like that
Gets the blood flowing
Makes it easier
to find a vein
You want an easy time
finding a vein
You don't want to be just
poking around
sticking yourself with the needle
trying to draw blood
That's a disaster
That's how mistakes get made

No, don't say anything
Now's not the time for talking
it's time for listening
Take the cotton out of your ears
and shove it in your mouth
You might actually learn something
if you shut that gaping cake hole
for five, fucking seconds

Now, this next part is embarrassing
but it's true, so you got to hear it
You're not going to be able to get it up
Once you shoot the dope
you blow any chance
of getting a hard on
Now, it's no big deal
because you won't have any interest in sex anyway
but your old lady might
so you're gonna have to think up some excuses
She might take your limp dick
as some kind of sign

that you're less than 100% red-blooded man
You know what I mean?
So think of some excuses
and they better be good
because it won't matter how she's going at you
either with her tits or her hand or her mouth
Nothing's gonna happen
All she's going to be holding
is two, scrawny inches
of squishy, flaccid uselessness

You understand what I'm saying?
You paying attention?
Don't be a smart ass
Wipe that shit-eating grin off your face
You think you're so smart
You're going to wish
you heeded my words
when you had the chance
If something bad happens to you
you won't think you're such a smart guy then

One last thing
Never shoot up
at your parent's house
or anywhere
near your kids
Dear God in Heaven
keep it away from your kids
This stuff can kill you
You know this shit can kill you, right?
Stop your heart
just like that
And when it does
it sure as Hell ain't pretty
and you don't want your parents

or, God forbid, your kids
finding your body
all smelly and bloated and dead
Am I right?
You bet your ass I'm right

It's the details, man
The details
are important
You gotta pay attention
to the details

A QUALITY OF MERCY

We played our punk rock records
on that old turn-table
with the worn-out needle
I gave greater value
than any other diamond

and you regaled me
with stories of men
worthier of your time than me

They made me sad
these stories
and they made me want to fuck you

desperately
and with such tender
love

which, I am certain
was always your intention
What better way to keep me
in your control?

"Where were these men?"
I wondered
Why weren't they here
instead of me?
It was only when I got older
that I came to understand
they had valued your
friction
much more than your
company

but as we danced and drank
and drank and danced
to Jello and Elvis and Sid
to Lou and Iggy and Patti
and smoked big, fat spliffs
of cheap tobacco mixed with pot
and danced and drank some more

you owned me
completely

Still, after all this time
I wish I could forgive you for your cruelty
and myself for my need
for when I picture your face
I mostly remember two things

the complete and total lack of joy
in your eyes when you smiled
and the burning hatred
that kept me warm
when you held me
in your arms

I suppose I ought to thank you
for letting me go

HOW TO BROACH THE SUBJECT OF ANAL WITH THE WOMAN OF YOUR DREAMS

gently now
avoid discomfort
by introducing the idea
a little at a time

we do not talk
//talk//not talk//
about what we want
//want//not want//
from each other

we expect to read
the expectations
in smile and grimace and wince
in whimper and groan
and sigh

slowly now
you could do damage
with an overwhelming
image

remember
to discuss
the need
//need//not need//
is to give it weight
to make it real
//real//not real//

ever so carefully
retract the suggestion
bit by bit

or it could hurt

someone

nothing is
forbidden
unless it is
forbidden

if you know
what I mean

SYMPATHY FOR THE DEALER

Indio was not a nice man
      he'd just as soon steal your wallet
      or fuck your girlfriend
      as sell you dope
but this was a business
of freaks and assholes
not nice men

He had the smack
      brown and sticky
      from Mexico or Guatemala
      ready to be melted down
and this was what mattered
not the quirks and deficiencies
of his rather loathsome personality

For the love of dope
we would gladly brave

      his filthy apartment
      that smelled of piss and vomit
      in which the grime
      seemed a thing alive
      coating a thick layer on the skin

For the love of dope
we would gladly brave

      his roaming, groping hands
      that would fall to rest
      seemingly absently
      on breasts or testicles
      and attempt a rote, clumsy caress

For the love of dope
we would gladly brave

        his fits of wild rage
        hands gesticulating madly
        and errant spittle
        undoubtedly infected with disease
        splashing off our faces

Indio was scum
        pure and simple scum
        straight junkie street trash
        one step up from the gutter
but he was our scum
and in a world like ours
this was all the distinction we needed

EVERYTHING'S MACBETH

> *I am in blood*
> *Stepp'd in so far, should I wade no more*
> *Returning were as tedious as go o'er*
> —MacBeth, William Shakespeare

The blood.
How do you change
the blood?
My rituals, though borne
from bloodletting,
so honest for that,
were selfish sacraments;
calling on gods
whose slumber was best
not to disturb.

There were prayers.
Yes, so many prayers;
invocations morning, noon and night.
Yet none to spare.
Even though, in the end
you needed them
far more than I,
I jealously hoarded them;
a nest egg of salvation.

Though I long to be different,
the past is a boulder,
weighing me down.
I've tried to purge
the man who abandoned you
but deceit runs in my veins.
In the end, it's always
the blood.
How do you change
the blood?

THE PATHOLOGY OF NEED AND NIGHT TRAIN

I was funny in my twenties
a jester fueled
by Southern Comfort and cheap jug wine
night after explosive night
winding up in
love or in jail
and you wouldn't have wanted it
any other way

I was something, wasn't I?
wild and feral and savage in my lust
for wine
for song
for experience

for you

but that was so long
so long ago

I curse you now
through broken teeth
and eyes clenched tight
fighting back the tears
that I refuse to shed
for your memory

damn you
for giving up
on me

The night train is coming now
coming down the tracks
and there's no one waiting

at the station anymore
but it's the only train I know

One by one
the friends have fallen away
to indifference and lives
rich and full, filled with work and family
that have no place for me
you were the last
and you stuck, bitterly, by my side
until you couldn't look at the man I am
and endure the comparison
to the man I used to be

The skin-tight jeans and whiskey glow
looked so goddamn sexy in my youth
but as I slide, definitively
over the hill
they are just a hardened shell
blocking out the light
and holding in the
rage

and even though I know it's going nowhere
when the night train comes for me
I always get on board

AT THE CAPITOL GARDEN MOTEL

I left my love for you, baby
at the Capitol Garden Motel
in a bare and dirty room
with an unmade bed
and shards of broken mirror
scattered on the rug
I hope you find it there
amid the crack-pipes and the needles
for I haven't the strength
to bring it back home to you

I miss you so much
that the loss of you
is hot, metal spikes
drilled through my brain
but I can't let you see me like this
and the last thing you need in your life
is an earthquake like me

I've been holed up for weeks
at the Capitol Garden Motel
with a sarcastic hooker
who only came for the coke
and can't remember my name
I wish you knew where to find me
because you've saved my life before
and though I've used up my chances
maybe you've got a little pity left
for old-time's sake and giggles

I wanted to love you, sweetheart
I really did but
I'm at my best
when lying and stealing and getting fucked up

so I can ape fidelity and loyalty
and sing hymns to your beauty
but I don't know what they mean

There isn't any garden
at the Capitol Garden Motel
only concrete and flop sweat
and the faded, distant echo
of happiness and hope
I can vaguely remember a man
who could have meant the world to you
but now I'm but a shadow
waiting for the light to fade
at the Capitol Garden Motel

I was somebody once

HOW TO EXPLAIN KARMA TO A SMALL CHILD

I was a germ
who dreamed it was a dragonfly
flitting from lily to lily
drinking in
the wind and the sun
stretching its wings
to the promise of
freedom

I was a dragonfly
who dreamed it was a dog
racing unfettered
through the meadow of flowers
shouting my name
to all who dare pass
I am here, I am here
you cannot deny
I am here

I was a dog
who dreamed it was a man
hunting for meat
tilling my field
punching the clock
in silent and solemn
parade
planting my flag
on hilltop, on desktop
on wife

I was a man
who dreamed he was
something
although he didn't know

quite what
something more and
something less
an aspiration, a goal
an idea
a germ
of an idea

I was a germ
who dreamed

1996

What became
of Justine?

We had nothing, you know
never loved
never fucked
never gave a damn at all

We shared a look
once or twice
of lust
of need
of hatred
That was all

Still, I wonder where she is
today

BEST LAID PLANS

i am going
    to leave you
to apologize
    to leave you
to back down
    to leave you
to tell you i was wrong

The first time that you hit me, I wanted, so badly, to hit you right back; to slap some sense into your stupid, fucking face. Later, we sat on the couch at your friend's house while you told me it was all my fault; that the words I used had pushed you into a corner and you had no other choice but to lash out; that I needed to be more careful about what I say to you; that you cannot be held responsible for your actions; that your wellbeing is my responsibility and that if I was a decent human being I would do anything in my power to keep you from losing control.

i am going
    to leave you
to bite my tongue
    to leave you
to walk on eggshells
    to leave you
to watch every word i say

Remember in the Disneyland parking lot, when you tried to hit me with that bottle of wine. You tried to kill me. That full bottle would, almost certainly, have crushed my skull. I had to grab your hand and wrestle the bottle away from you. You were screaming like a banshee and shaking like a leaf. I looked in your eyes but I couldn't see you at all. There was a stranger there. And you told me this was my fault too. That I made the mistake of standing up for myself and telling you what I wanted. I should have known better and it was perfectly reasonable of you to try to kill me.

i am going
> to leave you

to shut down
> to leave you

to roll into a ball
> to leave you

to swallow my feelings

Then that time we went camping. We had a nice time until the sun went down and you said something about communism and I made the mistake of telling you that you were wrong. It was my fault, I know. I should have known better than to contradict you. Of course, something like that is going to make you fly off the handle. You were perfectly within your rights to pick up that knife and try to stab me in the neck. I'm only sorry that I was so weak that I had to stop you and pry the knife out of your hand. If I had been a good person, I would have just taken my punishment like I deserved. It was my fault. My fault.

i am not going
> to leave you

to complain
> to leave you

to protect myself
> to leave you

fuck up again

i promise
baby

SEX OR SUICIDE

Pinning your hands
down to the bed

titillating terrorism

to hold you so
enthralled

Is this the way you want it?

Sooner or later
one of us
will apologize

probably me
probably me

but not before
the damage
is done

black eyes and bruised pride
broken bottles held at throats
curses screamed and a touch of blood
to color the proceedings

We are engaged
in this struggle
you and I
but what to name it?

Is it sex
or is it suicide?

THERE AIN'T EPIPHANY ENOUGH FOR THAT

If you look real hard
you can almost see
the razor blades and broken promises
in my crooked smile

What did Lou call it?
In New York?
The Statue of Bigotry, right?
Crude, I know
but oh so real

You can try to tell me
my experience
Mr. Weekend-born-again
but when I'm down on my knees
with a dick in my mouth
and an eight ball in my pocket
my faith in sweet, lord Jesus
is every ounce as strong
as yours

You and I
are not afraid to die
It's life
that keeps us up at night
love
that gives us nightmares

THE LIE

I had to tell it
the lie
I had to
It was either
the lie
or my life
That's how I saw it
You've got to understand
I had no choice
It's not my fault
I had to tell it
the lie

The odds were not
in my favor
and the dice
they came up snake eyes
every time
If it wasn't for bad luck
I'd have no luck at all

I sat at the table
in the restaurant
surrounded by family
celebrating some shit
or some other shit
who the hell knows?
Starting to get sick
feeling the sweat
slowly dripping
down my back
soaking my shirt
making me stick
to the cheap, vinyl chair
Any moment now

the shakes would come

So I needed to find
something
a lie
to get me out of there
a lie
that I could tell
to find some privacy
away from those eyes
where I could slip in the needle
in peace

A black cloud hung over me
following me around
surrounding me
choking my lungs
raining
on my parade
my parade
of fashionable suicide

I tried the bathroom
the fucking bathroom
but it was no bathroom at all
not for my needs
no doors on the stalls
Who makes a bathroom
with no doors on the stalls?
Who wants to shit
in full view?
Who wants to do
what I had to do
where people could see?
I can't shoot dope
where people can see

So I had to tell it
the lie
I had to
I had no choice
It was either my life
or the lie
That's how I saw it
I'm not ashamed
I had to do it
I'd do it again
tell the lie
again
if I had to

But it had to be good
to be foolproof
had to get me out of there
out of the restaurant
away from the eyes
away
from my family
my entire, fucking family
make it so
no one would follow
make it so
no one would ever want
to follow

So I told them
the lie
the best lie
I could come up with
that I had hemorrhoids
that I had shit myself
that I had to go back
back to the car
to clean myself up

that was the lie
and no one would question me
no one would follow me
now
It was either the lie
or my life
my quickly fading life
That's how I saw it

because I'm a junkie
a hopeless, street hype
I need what I need
and that's more important
than family

than dignity

So I told them
the lie
I had to
to protect them
from the truth
They don't want to know
the truth
That's why I told them
the lie
and someday soon

tomorrow
or the next day
or the day after that

they'll stop believing
but until they do
I'll just keep telling
the lie

WALLS ARE THIN

The walls are thin
and the couple fucking
in the purgatory next door
is making my teeth rattle
with the insistence of their ardor
or maybe it's the crank I've been shooting
for nigh on a week now
That's probably a more logical explanation
but I'm not known
for my logic

The walls are thin, though
as thin as my skin
and if I touch the place on my ego
where the things you said about me live,
long enough and with sufficient pressure,
then the pain is so intense and
erotic

I deserve this
all of it
this room
with its Mexican fiesta vomit bedspread
its rape of Nanking wallpaper
its paper thin walls
and your disdain, your disinterest, your derision
I am a rank and rotting
Spam sculpture of a man

No one knows that
better than
the woman next door
fucking her nameless partner
with such brutal, clinical precision

grunting in time
to the drip of my tears

You never made that sound
when you were with
me

WASTED LIFE

Bambi looked at me one day in March
and the crooked, broken smile on her face
and the house-on-fire terror in her eyes
made me pull myself
inch by inch
from my long and wintry deep dope nod
to give her every, little bit
of my usually scattershot attention

She said,
"You know, man,
a wasted life
is better
than no life at all."

She fell silent for an instant after that
and I stared at her, quizzically
trying to make sense of her statement
and the macabre combination
of hysterical laughter
and gut-wrenching sobs
that followed

Had she been talking about drugs
or hinting at something deeper
sadder
more profound?

She was in no condition to explain, however
shaking as she was
from the amalgamation
of guffaws and tears
but I've never forgotten her words
or the faint suspicion

that what she was really doing
was begging for my help

and as I drifted back
to my crushed velvet oblivion
I caught myself
wiping a single tear from my face
and thinking,
"Next time she looks for a savior
I hope she can find one
just a little less
wasted."

ONE DROP OF MILK

Don't cry
over spilled milk, scream
over spilled milk, rage
at the imperfection

Control
your surroundings
if you can, control
your wife, your children
for the things that really matter
are out of your
control

There is a certain way
that things are supposed to be
There are certain feelings
we're supposed to feel
that look good
that look right
that look normal
to the outside world

You could be a killer
You could be a rapist
You could be a pervert
as long as you go to church
and sang your hymns
and paid your tithes

along with all the other
upstanding killers
and horny holy men

and drink your milk

all your milk
one drop out of place
will spoil this delicate
balance

Don't make any waves
Don't spill any milk
We prefer the neat and tidy box
you are pretending to be
to the mess you are
inside

You are only ever
one drop of milk
from the truth

One drop of milk
can give you away

PASSING THE TORCH

I can't remember his name.
Was it Tony? Or Timmy? I don't know.
He just wanted a taste
of the oblivion I had found
in the spoon, the needle, the syringe,
and he was old enough
to choose for himself.

That's what I told myself, that
it wasn't my responsibility
to teach him right and wrong;
that if it hadn't been me,
then some other schmo
would have taken his gentle hand
and led him to the limbo land.

And he was eager, oh so eager,
to lose himself a little;
to blur the edges between
the man he was and
the man he wanted to be,
and I knew the way, the code,
the secret language of the night.

So, with the kit between my teeth,
I placed his arm upon my legs,
tied him off above the elbow
and, after giving him a look that said,
"Don't worry my friend,
this will be easier than you think,"
I slid the twilight in.

And Tony, or Timmy, or whatever his name
took to this purgatory

the way our kind always do.
He wore it like a blanket
and he chased it like a dream,
till it was the only thought he could conceive
when he woke up in the morning
and when he went to bed at night.

I can't remember his name.
Was it Tony? Or Timmy? I can't recall,
and I have no idea what's become
of him, whether he's alive or dead
or if he's in prison or walking free
but I wish I could see him
one more time, so I could ask him
to forgive me, for passing
my loathsome torch to him

WORDS SPOKEN, AND WORDS LEFT UNSAID

As she was walking out the door
I looked at her eyes, still wet with tears
and I told her I loved her, even though
I had no idea what those words meant
They were just words, spoken in hope
of relieving my guilt the tiniest bit

We had something between us
some emotional super glue
creating an airtight bond
holding us together
but you couldn't call it love

How can you love someone
and ask them to do
the things I knew she was doing
to keep us from getting sick?
To keep us high?

She had lied to me
telling me she was only stripping
only taking off her clothes
that it hadn't gone any further
that it wouldn't go any further
They would never be allowed
to touch, to debase, to spoil
and I, in turn, lied to myself
that I believed
she was telling the truth

But what was there to do?

I watched her go and I tried to yell,
"Stop. Don't go. You don't need to do this.

We'll find another way. We'll beat this thing.
You and me. Together."
That's what I should have said
What I would have said

had I loved her

but no sound came out of
my open mouth and in the end
I shut the door and let her walk away

THIS SPACE

You are here

in every corner
under
every floor mat and seat cushion
filling
every crevice and pore

You are on me
around me
filling the air
informing the dust
singing
at the top of your lungs
this space

that smile
that melts so easily
melts on me
smile a highway
between space
and this space

The table we live at
the shitty, balsa wood molding
the weight of the air
and sleeping dogs
snoring with safety and pride
all drip you
they bleed you
they know your holy name
in the fiber

of this space

ALIENATION SONGS

Send me your love
as rousing anthems of alienation
you beautiful freaks of nature
sailing in a glass-bottom boat
on the deep and restless sea
of fluid sexuality and gender
You are who you want to be
or at least who you say you are
It's not my right to judge
I will take you at face value
once I cut through
the running mascara and caked on blush
to lay my fingers on your real face

Kiss me your strength
with the red lips of rejection
you weird and wild children
running through the glass and metal jungle
aping the apes
with stand-up, slapstick semaphore
You are manifestos writ in flesh
Or, at least in spilling blood
It is not my place to say
I will pull you to my chest
as soon as I determine
which are your tentacles?
Which are your arms?

Sing me your souls
as lilting hymns of sass and sorrow
you dark and damaged vessels
writing your anguish and angst
on perfumed stationary
that you leave as suicide notes

to mystify your parents
You are less than you desire
yet much more than you seem
Who am I to name you?
I will gladly listen to your stories
as soon as I begin to separate
the concrete from the moss

DEATH WATCH

You hold her hand, my love
as she drifts away from you
to a place
you cannot follow.

How many times and through
how many trials
have you held this hand before?

Yet, it's different this time
colder, more hollow
and her fingers shake
from the shock of the new

from the abyss
of the possible

And I wish I could caress your face
or hold her hand for you
so you don't have to feel
what we both know
you must feel

For only you know her
with such intimate kisses
and alone you can touch her
with the names
of her family, of her friends
of her regrets

It won't be long now
and then the tears will spill
like the blood
that flows between you

between you and her

You'll never be more lovely
than when your heart is torn in two

LONG WINTER

His sated penis
recoils and retreats
from the icy cold of his fingers
while a thick veil of steam
rises from his cascade of piss
fogging the mirror
With his free hand
he writes in the fog,
"It's only one more day."

He'd fucked her an apology
much better than flowers
longer lasting, more satisfying
At least that's what she tells him
and she knows damn well
not to lie to his face
There's a penalty for that
He doesn't have time
to make reparations again

On his way to the door
he pauses to examine her
lying, listlessly, on the bed
The fresh welts are red and angry
a testament to his passion
or to his drunkenness the night before
he can't remember which
"Either way," he thinks,
"she probably deserved it."

Turning the locks on the door
he can't resist one last look
She has turned her head
To regard him, as if he were a bug

"Is that condescension or hate
in her eyes?" he wonders
He spreads his trained monkey smile to her
then walks out the door
Some things are better not to know

COCK AND CONSEQUENCE

My dick is flying
at half mast
to commemorate your memory

I've tried to raise it
to the sky
to announce my independence
But this
is as high
as it will go

I've rubbed the damn thing
RAW
and still
your name
will not wipe off

My dick appears
determined
to act as the barometer
to my soul

Oh, how I long
for a bottle of whiskey
and a sharp pair
of scissors
to rid myself
of this troublesome bother
once and for all

PITY

He lured me in with promises
of sweet Humboldt weed and cold brewskis
(yes, this was the '70s and I was 14)
and, to be fair, he lived up
to that part of the bargain
He just neglected to mention
what he had planned for later

If I am to despise you
in your weakness
I must also hate my own
so what else can I feel

but pity?

I never knew his name
(or maybe I've blocked it out)
but he was a middle-aged man
going to fat and losing his hair
and before he was finished
he had crumbled in tears
showing me pictures of the wife and kids
he had at home
and explained this was something
he felt compelled to do

Oh, he was wrong
of course he was wrong
but don't we all hide
some hidden shame
we fear to show?
Couldn't we all do
with a little

pity?

He had a Chevy van
(if the van's a rockin', don't come a knockin')
that was perfect for his needs
private and comfortable
with cushions everywhere and curtains on the windows
to discourage prying eyes
for the games he had in mind to play there
were not the kind he'd want the world to see

No doubt he was warped and broken
but take a good look around you
Aren't we all?
Maybe what could hold us together
is just a tiny bit

of pity

He waited till I was very buzzed
before he slid his hands down my pants
(to be honest, I'd never felt any hands there
except for my own)
but I pushed him away with all my strength
and lashed out with fingernails, teeth
whatever I had to defend myself
He didn't fight back, though
just collapsed to his knees
begging for my forgiveness
and, perhaps,
for his own

In the end
I couldn't give him my body
but I held his head
to my chest

and listened to him weep
as I gave him

a lethal dose of

my pity

THE SPIRITUAL DERIVATION OF THE WORD "FUCK"

There have been entire books written
about the warm, electric charge that happens
when you grab my ass while we're fucking and

we're fucking and

we're fucking and

not I'm fucking you or
you're fucking me but

we're fucking and

let's face it, kids
religions have been founded
simply to deny that this feeling exists
Christ, ain't that all religions?
Well, maybe not Scientology
Who the hell knows what that is?
But when my cock is hard
so hard that it makes me feel
like I can never, ever die and
it's inside of you
not just your pussy
it's you, inside of you, all of you and
eyes locked, breathing in unison
so that we can't tell
if it's yours or mine or ours or
something entirely new and
your hands slide up the backs of my legs and
squeeze as hard as they can so that
I can't suppress the giggle that
begins there in my ass and
travels the length of my body before

escaping as bliss from my throat and

we're fucking and

we're fucking and

we're fucking and

I want to write a book about it too that
will destroy all religion
once and for all
forever and ever but
I realize the book is redundant
We are that book and
no religion could ever exist
in a moment this pure
this right
this connected
Can I get an amen?
Can I get an amen?
Say it with me please
Say it loud and say it proud
God is love and love is God and

we're fucking and

we're fucking and

we are love and love is we and
God is love and
we
are
God

And people say
that fuck's a dirty word

DON'T GO AWAY

You are standing
right in front of me
but you're not there
at least, not completely

There are frustrating flashes
of the person
you used to be
like you are hidden
behind a broken fence
and, for an instant
you can be seen clearly
only to suddenly
be obscured again

Please remember
my name
Please remember
our history
Please remember
what we've been through
together

The separate pieces of my life
have all been stitched into meaning
by shared experience
with you

You are my glue

When you are gone
what will hold me
together?

You are the sand
in an hourglass
and I'm watching you
slip away

Today, my name
still fell from your lips
and your eyes touched mine
with recognition
with warmth
but what will be left
tomorrow?

Please, Father
Please, Mother
Please stay with me here
a little bit longer

Don't leave me like this
all alone and lonely

Don't go away

ALLOW ME TO BREAK THE FOURTH WALL AND SPEAK TO YOU, THE READER, DIRECTLY

If I pour
all the pain in my soul
into my Facebook status
and nobody "likes" it
have I really said anything?
do I really exist
at all?

I need your validation
can you hear me?
can you see me?
am I invisible?
is this all
for nothing?

I put myself
naked and unafraid
into every single word
only to watch those words
one by one in an endless cycle
disappear
into the void
never to be heard from
again

What good is my anger
my rage, my fists slamming
against the walls
of the here and now
when my life and my vocation
is for keeping you
calm?

Am I still standing
on the treadmill, spinning
my wheels?
Or am I just a memory
of me?
one last electrical impulse
before I fade
into the stratosphere?

It's so hard to grow up
when you're already
old

BUSY FUCKING THE RAT GIRL

I was busy
fucking the rat girl
so I could hold at bay
the creeping, nagging suspicion
of my total worthlessness
that rejection had left
that your rejection
had left

She and I dropped acid together, on her dirty mattress, putting the dropper on each other's tongues till the room began to spin and strange faces poured out of the laundry basket, while the rat girl's rat danced around our naked genitals and nibbled at our fingertips, drawing the blood that we needed for our rituals of debasement.

Maybe if she let me
this little rat girl
I could fuck away the pain
fuck away the heartbreak
fuck away the shame
fuck away all my bothersome
personality, I could fuck away
myself

We fucked up and down the 101, the rat girl and I, going from Humboldt to Frisco to LA, over one Christmas in limbo, where we must have been trying to outrun what was best for us, fucking all the way, we fucked in a Sauna in Sausalito, in a $2 hotel in the Castro, at her friend's house in Sacramento, fucked at an ex-girlfriends place in Silverlake, at the Exploratorium near the Presidio and in her parents bed in Novato, we tried to fill up the days with fucking so they couldn't fill themselves with thinking.

and maybe if she let me
this darling little rat girl
I could fuck hard enough and fast enough and frenetically enough
that I wouldn't see your face
I wouldn't see your face
I wouldn't see your face
when I closed my eyes at night

She wasn't the rat girl because there was anything wrong with her, goodness no, she was sweet, she was wonderful, she was a good girl, she deserved better than me, she was the rat girl because of her rat, whose name I can never remember, it was Steve or Darrell or Monty or something like that, that rode around on her shoulder day and night, everywhere she went, that sat by my head and stared into my eyes every time I was fucking her, fuck, I hate rats.

Now, no one wants to be the rat girl
a talisman
against self-pity
a stop-gap or a stand-in
holding place in line
for when true love comes calling
unless you're too busy
fucking

The rat girl was bald and rode around in an electric wheelchair, I guess she was a punker, that's what she said and what I told myself and she sure did like to fuck, morning, noon and night but there's nothing wrong with that and I liked to think that I must be some hot shit, since she wanted to fuck me all the time, that I must be extra sexy or lovable but I was really just her opium, the same as she was for me.

I would have seen my life
flashing in front of my eyes

if I hadn't been busy
busy fucking
the rat girl

TO THE GIRL WITH ARMAGEDDON IN HER EYES

Everybody wants to kill themselves
when the last line of coke is gone
we're all armed with razor blades
to ward off the rising of the sun
and it wouldn't be living, would it
if we ever went to bed
before the rest of the world punched the clock?

but I can taste the blood in your smile
and smell the burning bodies
in the way your shoulders slump
so don't think you're something special
there's a wasteland
in your weathered face
and why not?
you know your lips
can't be half as sweet
as you've been advertising

Who are we to keep our chins up
when everyone around us
falls so far short
of who we need them to be

'Cause everybody wants to kill themselves
when they down the final slug from the bottle
and have to chew the worm
with teeth, gritted and rigid
from too many nights without sleep
too many days in robotic motion
watching every movement
every fantasy of death and torture
making damn sure they're still trapped
inside our heads and not loose

wreaking havoc in the here and now

but I can read the disappointment
that clearly shows between the letters
of your coerced confession
so don't expect any special treatment
there's a civil war
between the soft words you say
and the inferno in your eyes
too bad you can't write "give's good blow jobs"
in the skill list on your résumé

We've got no right to be judgmental
when the only thing we've ever built
with our own two hands
are the shackles on our feet

And everybody wants to kill themselves
when they discover the ocean
cannot wash their sins away
and when they must hide themselves
back in the closet
only moments after they've emerged

And everybody wants to kill themselves
when they come to realize
that candy cannot offer consolation
and Judy Garland
never really lived in Kansas

And everybody wants to kill themselves
when they wake up in the morning
and look in the mirror

And everybody wants to kill themselves
when they cannot go to sleep

at night

Yet here we are
giddy with survival
deliriously tongue-tied
with the promise
of tomorrow

LOUSY BOUNCER

Absently watching the blood
drip, languidly, to the dirty floor
burgundy pools of memory
shattered bone and hope
picking bits of broken teeth
from my ruined fingers

When I was thirteen
I was a middle-aged man
cursing the cruel world
and the stupidity of people
a suburban Caligula
wishing all the talking heads of my youth
could have only one neck

Does that whiskey look like sex to me
or is it just the boredom talking?
I've been on the wagon so long
I can't remember what it tastes like
but I can't forget the morning after
the hot knives behind my eyes
and the humid, sultry taste
like candy-coated, rotting meat
I couldn't wash from my mouth

When I was twenty-three
I was a dying old fart
wishing I'd never seen your eyes
and praying that your voice
would get out of my fucking head
It never occurred to me
breathing in and out
in this asthmatic limbo
that I just hadn't met you yet

Don't try your stories on me brother
I've heard them all before
or variations of the same
and my hatred grows exponentially
with each reason or excuse given
as to why your case is different
and you deserve to be let in for free
Maybe I'll just start cracking heads
and let God sort it out
When I was thirty-two
I was a memory
there was nothing of me left
for you to hang onto
had you even desired to
My skin hung from my bones
like a going-out-of-business sale
You, at least, had the courage and compassion
to leave my fate to others
wallowing in my own filth and pity

Pay no attention to the broken nose
the split lip and sunken cheeks
I'm as handsome as I've ever been
or ever hoped to be
but then, as we both know
I set the bar low
and my expectations even lower
I imagine that on this very date
a thousand years from now
I might be almost ready and willing
to take a look in the mirror

CRIMINAL

Breaking in
is easier than it looks
a twist of the crowbar, a kick
anyone can do it
but not anyone will
it takes a

criminal

because only a

criminal has nothing to lose
only a
criminal has walled off his trust
only a
criminal sings heartbreak to the morning

Embezzling is
just fudging the numbers
and everybody knows
that numbers don't need to be tortured
they don't need to be seduced
numbers will tell you
anything you want them to
and they'll be happy to do it
Numbers like to say no
but they really mean yes

You'd never know that
unless you're a

criminal

because only a

criminal is a desolate church
only a
criminal is an uncharted island
only a
criminal is a homeless bird
trying to find its nest

Murder in
the first degree is
difficult the first time
but gets much easier
with every chance for practice
get creative with the pain
it is the only gift you know
but this can be felt
only by a

criminal

because only a

criminal has been tutored in misery
only a
criminal has foreclosed his compassion
only a
criminal has memorized loyalty

for I am only a

criminal

at least, that's what you taught me
that's what you called me
that's what you named me
and only a

criminal

would lie about that

wouldn't he?

THE GRACES OF DIAN

She wouldn't tell me
what she thought of me
that was the first thing
I had been dreading that information
but she flashed her police brutality smile
which gave me a pretty telling clue

The second was when
she smashed that record
the one that we'd danced to
in the summer of '89
when it seemed like love was real
and kisses tasted
like rebellion
I would never need to listen
to the little broken shards

I guess the third
was when she fucked her way
through my high school yearbook
By the time she was finished
she had chipped away
at my list of defenders
which had not been so long to begin with
leaving no witnesses
to my surrender

SEARCHING FOR JESUS (ON THE WORLD.WIDE.WEB)

waking up
with an erection
should i beat it
or just let it die?
and if she were
to take me in her mouth
would this be too much
to ask?

this I trust
the veiny steel of my dick
the cold, gamey spunk
on the sheets
the flash of memorized shame
that surely follows
all else is sophistry

i've looked for you
in paintings and song
in churches and children
and trees
in mass murderers and shopping malls
in television talk shows
and traffic accidents
and in the prayers
of the people i love

but you're not there

if I could find
the perfect combination of words
and Google them
with the right amount
of purity and delicacy

maybe then
i could believe
in you?

DIANE'S FIRST ABORTION

Sitting in the waiting room, waiting
for Diane's first abortion,
hands wringing, knuckles cracking, foot tapping,
keeping time to the beat
of the shame.

It had been scrambling and
writhing, in the back of the car,
buttons popped, clothing torn,
semen, ejaculated quickly and spilling
slowly down her leg.

It had been terror and
tears, both parent and child,
screaming disappointment and
apology, promising penance,
begging God for reprieve.

It had been selfishness and
self-pity, cursing the failure
of condom and pill, whining,
"Why me? Oh, why me?
Why must it be me?"

and in all the excitement
who had the time to consider
the baby, who would be
never named

or mentioned again?

GREAT MOMENTS IN SILENCE

There is a number to call
1-800-something-something
if you absolutely must
complain
about gay marriage
or that some people
get to choose
their own gender

Join my campaign
against soup
because if God had intended
soup
he/she/it wouldn't have scattered
the ingredients
he/she/it would have fucking miracled
soup
already made
and hot

Maybe
we're a disease
maybe
technology is nature
maybe
everything
is natural

MEMENTO MORI

There's so much hair
in the shower
      her hair
little razor-wire reminders
spun gold souvenirs
of a better time

She's been gone for a month now
even her scent
has been bleached from the bedding
yet still her hair
remains

clogging up the drain
holding in the

hatred

LINDA'S CHOICE

She told me she was horny.
"I'll fuck anything that moves," she said
So, I tried to remain
perfectly still.

I was tired to the bone
and I wasn't in the mood
to be human OxyContin
or play father confessor
with my dick.

She needed this discomfort
more than she needed my semen.
Pain was her professor now,
stern and unyielding, to be sure
but so much more potent for that.

"You've begged for it before,"
she chided me
and I had, at that,
on my back or on my knees,
whimpering and pleading,
"I just want to be loved."

Christ, don't we all
but it doesn't work like that.
Love isn't the hands
that fondle our bodies.
it's the blood
we mop up off the floor.

It's the wounds we decline
to look away from.

So, I turned to her and said,
"I'll give you a choice.
I could fuck you now
and that will be the end,
or I could love you forever,
with my mind, with my heart, with my words."

She threw her head back
with a hearty laugh and told me,
"That's sweet, little man,
but you just ain't that special.
I guess I'll have to choose
the sex."

I leaned in
to kiss Linda gently on the lips
and with a sigh
I started to undress.

ACID AND YOU AND ALLEN GINSBERG

First dates are awkward at best
the desire to fuck wedged uncomfortably
against the need to make small talk
but we circumvented that difficulty
with a little Orange Sunshine on the tongue

and we let the fireworks begin

I don't remember the drive
did you drive? did I drive?
Yet somehow, we arrived
in one piece, in Santa Monica
to watch Allen Ginsberg pump
his harmonium all night
like he was playing tug-of-rope with my dick

and my dick was hard
mysteriously, embarrassingly
in the club, watching Ginsberg
and later, at Scott's apartment
in the shower with you

with you
hands on my body
lips on my body
flesh on my flesh
and we agreed, telepathically, to pretend
that my erection
and everything that was to issue from it
would belong to you
on that night
and for the foreseeable future

You dubbed me conquest

and I named you Crumb Queen
as we writhed, naked, on the floor
and your friend slept innocently
in the room next door

At one pristine point
my penis entered
into unholy congress with you
Or I could have just imagined that
like I imagined the seraphim and cherubim
dancing 'round my head
singing "Walk on the Wild Side"

Doo doo doo doo doo doo doo doo doo
Doo doo doo doo doo doo doo doo doo
Doo doo doo doo doo doo doo doo doo
Doo doo doo doo doo doo doo doo doo
Doo doo doo doo doo doo doo doo doo
Doo doo doo doo doo doo doo doo doo
Doo doo doo doo doo doo doo doo doo doo

and I fell in love
if not with you
then at least with the possibility
of my own freedom

I'm sorry if I made you promises
I never meant to keep
but I'm sure Ginsberg would have smiled broadly
if he could have looked on us that night

Other Titles by This Author

Junkies Die Alone
Five Words that Can Cripple a Man
I'll ONly Write Poems for You
Everyone is Broken

MAX MUNDAN is a poet, an author, a wild animal photographer, and a lover of freedom in all its wild forms. He lives with his amazing wife and two charming dogs on the road in an RV. He is the author of four previous collections of poetry, including "I'll Only Write Poems for You," which was released by Weasel Press in November 2016. Max has also gathered a large following(as well as a large group of angry trolls) for his political writing that has been featured in Thought Catalog and The Inquisitr.

Other Titles from Weasel Press

Pan's Saxophone by Jonel Abellanosa
Hyper-Real Reboots by Sudeep Adhikari
despair is a mandelbrot set by Sudeep Adhikari
Wayward Realm by Sendokidu Adomi
Ghost Train by Matt Borczon
To Burn in Torturous Algorithms by Heath Brougher
Klonopin Meets Sisyphus by Adam Levon Brown
The House of Eros by Matthew David Campbell
Harmonious Anarchy by Matthew David Campbell
H A I L by Stanford Cheung
Still Life Over Coffee by Robert Cone
The Madness of Empty Spaces by David E. Cowen
The Seven Yards of Sorrow by David E. Cowen
Bleeding Saffron by David E. Cowen
Face Down in the Leaves by Dwale
Wine Country by Robin Wyatt Dunn
Smash & Grab Poems by Ryan Quinn Flanagan
In Winter's Dreams We Wake by Ryan Quinn Flanagan
If the Hero of Time was Black by Ashley Harris
Dormant Volcano by Ken Jones
Email Epistles by Ken Jones
Evergreen by Sarah Frances Moran
I Am A Terrorist by Sarah Frances Moran
Blame it On the Texas Sky by Max Mundan
I'll Only Write Poems for You by Max Mundan
Rising from the Ashes by Meghan O'Hern
Lipstick Stained Masculinity by Mason O'Hern
Chaos Songs by Scott Thomas Outlar
Kisses and Kickflips by Kacey Pinkerton
In Another Life, Maybe by Michael Prihoda
the first breath you take after giving up by Michael Prihoda
the same that happened yesterday by Michael Prihoda
Beneath this Planetarium by Michael Prihoda
Years without Room by Michael Prihoda

Toast is Just Bread that Put Up A Fight by Emily Ramser
I forgot How To Write When They Diagnosed Me by Emily Ramser
Conjuring Her by Emily Ramser
UHAUL: A Collection of Lesbian Love Poems by Emily Ramser
The Escape by Rayah
Taste & See by Neil S. Reddy
Inevitable by Amy L. Sasser
Satan's Sweethearts by Marge Simon and Mary Turzillo
We Don't Make It Out Alive by Weasel
Cut the Loss by Weasel
Colliding with Orion by Chris Wise
Cuentos de Amor by Z.M. Wise
Wolf: An Epic and Other Poems by Z.M. Wise
Kosmish and the Horned Ones by Z.M. Wise
Ghostly Pornographers by Thomas White

www.ingramcontent.com/pod-product-compliance
Lightning Source LLC
Chambersburg PA
CBHW051654040426
42446CB00009B/1127